Buddha on a Bike

Stories of an enlightened cyclist-wannabe

Bodhisattva won't you take me by the hand?

-Steely Dan

Contents

Foreword   by Ken O'Neil

Prologue

Chapter 1 Contrasting Pairs

Chapter 2 Diligence

Chapter 3 Mind

Chapter 4 Flowers

Chapter 5 The Childish Person

Chapter 6 The Skilled Person

Chapter 7 The Accomplished Person

Chapter 8 Thousands

Chapter 9 Detriment

Chapter 10 Violence

Chapter 11 Old Age

Chapter 12 Oneself

Chapter 13 The World

Chapter 14 The Awakened

Chapter 15 Being at Ease

Chapter 16 Pleasing

Chapter 17 Anger

Chapter 18 Toxins

Chapter 19 Firmly on the Way

Chapter 20 The Path

Chapter 21 Scattered Themes

Chapter 22 The Lower World

Chapter 23 Elephant

Chapter 24 Craving

Chapter 25 The Practitioner

Chapter 26 The Superior Person

Foreword

As any seasoned veteran knows, peak performance is a slow, non-linear process marked by continuity of just doing it, to the point where neurotic illusions of becoming a super hero are offset by embracing an almost love/hate relationship with daily training, daily doing, daily effort. And emptying oneself of any concerns and agendas other than gaining concentrated focus on right now, this workout, this session. Maybe hoping for that occasional breakthrough until it's learned in the heart those occasional breakthroughs aren't guaranteed, that at best they seem like accidents. At that point, training moves from neurotic obsession with outcomes to developing a deep presence in making oneself accident prone with respect to those rare, non-linear breakthroughs that change our lives, waking us up to the next horizon of training. Embrace plateaus — they're the progressive stages. Periodization establishes continuity (tantra). Character emerges. Frank's tales of cycling bode well for more than bicycles. All training is cyclical. Buddha on a Bike alternatively is Awakening on a bike, awakening in cycles. Savor each story not as a stand-alone, but joyfully as threaded tales of progressively deepening insights, the continuity warp and woof of self-disclosure. Frank strikes a vein of pure gold with this amazing book. His disclosure is of wisdom earned by mistakes, misgivings, preconceptions, over training, under training, all the things we have to engage in to gain self-mastery. In that respect, Frank's a need breed Dharma-master of a post-monastic, naturalistic humanism brewing as the next step in deliberately disclosing survival of the wisest.

Ken O'Neil

Prologue

I first began riding a bike as a kid. Great fun, transportation to school and eventually a means of independence on any given Saturday. I would start out early and get home just before dark after covering a good portion of the town I lived in. But as most young men will attest, the bike gave way to a car and for many years I did not ride. After college and a few years of marriage, my wife and I embarked on a trip of a lifetime. Selling our home in Northwest Colorado we put all of our belongings in storage (including the car) and took off on a bicycle adventure covering the western part of the U.S. We were on our bikes for 61 days with stories that will, perhaps fill the pages of another book one day.

I was introduced to bicycle racing by a friend who is part of one of the stories in this book. It was an auspicious beginning but in some shape or form it entered into my life in a big way. So much so, it remains today. During this period of my involvement with a bicycle the focus was on training and competition. Group rides and training protocols that were designed to improve my fitness and move me closer to the finish line against my competitors. As I continued to train, I began to realize that the time I spent on the bicycle was a gift. A gift I gave myself by scheduling a ride each day to not only improve my fitness, but to allow me some perspective on the issues surrounding my life. The concerns associated with work, home life and considerations of all things spiritual and philosophical, seemed to surface for scrutiny during my bike rides. Problems were solved, issues were resolved and my relationship with a higher power was fostered. I often remarked to my friends and family, that my bike rides were my spiritual refuge. They still are.

    I began writing my bicycling adventure stories with the purpose of somehow matching the meaning within each story to a spiritual truth. As I wrote, I was not sure which spiritual truth or what spiritual truth I would match my stories to but I kept writing, assured in the belief that I would one day find a match. I had written 25 stories of distinction and impact, all the while knowing I had more in my memory but also realizing I did not want to be redundant…as many rides tend to be. I was at an impasse.

    I happened upon a book on the verses of "The Way" from the teachings of The Buddha. Dhammapada is a guide, a translation, a prescription of the Buddha's teachings. There are 26 chapters or teachings in the Dhammapada. I have taken select verses from these teachings for this book. I ask the reader to forgive me for my ignorance in Buddhism as well as any possible misinterpretation of the selected verses. I continue to learn on my own path. What is interesting in my finding these verses is not only the complete match in number (26 chapters, 25 stories) but the ease at which each select verse from each chapter tells the essence of the meaning within my bicycle stories. The matching was so complete, that the 26th chapter of the Dhammapada was saved for my last story which I easily formulated upon completing the reading of the last chapter. But there is a more interesting context I have realized and feel compelled to inform the reader of as it pertains to these verses and my stories.

After matching my bicycling stories to these select verses within chapters of Buddhist teachings, I believe that each and every story could be switched with many if not all the verses of the teachings. I will even go so far as to say I believe I could have accomplished the same thing had I chosen the teachings of Jesus, or Krishna or Mohammad. I believe this because I believe these stories are not just my stories of bicycling adventures, but stories of everyday life. While these particular stories may be unique to my path, their meaning resonates throughout humanity in many different scenarios. My stories are your stories. These lessons are our lessons to be shared. In that context, I hope this book provides you insight into our shared condition we know as life.

Dr. Frank B. Wyatt

Contrasting Pairs: Chapter 1

*In this world
hostilities are never
appeased by hostility.
But by the absence of hostility
are they appeased.
This is an interminable truth.*

*Although reciting many religious texts,
if one does not practice accordingly,
he is a heedless man.
Like a cowherd counting the cows of others,
he has no share in the religious life.*

*Although reciting but little from religious texts,
if one is good, he lives in harmony with the teachings.
Abandoning passion, hatred, and delusion,
he possesses proper understanding, perfect purity of mind
Showing no attachment to this world or beyond,
he has a share in the religious life.*

Story 1: Most of the time a cyclist spends on his/her bike is during training. But this story takes place during a race. It was an unusual race in Colorado in that it began at 7000 ft. and ended on the top of a mountain, Mt. Evans at 14,000 ft. Unlike most road races that begin rather slowly and have an ebb and flow to them, this race began hard and only got harder. It was not enough that an individual could just race to finish first in this climb, but records to the top were pursued each year. So as I stated, the race began with a blistering pace. What was not unusual for a mid-July race was a bit of precipitation as we started. This actually cooled us during the hard drive toward the forever climb. As with any race, encountering a long climb, as the road went up, the riders strung out. And soon I found myself in that area referred to as "no-mans land". The place between those that dropped you and those you have dropped. I was all alone. Above timberline the temperatures dropped and soon I noticed a smattering of snow-flakes. Turning yet another corner the snow picked up and before long, it was a full blown white-out. Leaving from 7000 ft. in the middle of summer, the only clothing I had to partially guard against this winter onslaught were arm warmers. But the snow began to accumulate on my arms as I constantly wiped my glasses for visibility. My teeth chattered as I continued to push the pedals in a survival mode to keep my body temperature elevated against the cold. I approached the final stretch which had a slight turn to the right, and the push to the finish line. Immediately arms and blankets were placed over me. I was escorted to our team van which had a heater and several other shivering cyclists fighting the hypothermia. It was quiet inside the van. No one spoke as our bodies gradually warmed to normal. Our minds tried to fathom the unusual environment we had just experienced. I caught a ride back down the mountain with a stranger that loaded my bike onto their rack. As they navigated the twists and turns of this mountain road I fell asleep from exhaustion as did the other three cyclists in the car. I put my bike on my car and drove the thirty minutes down to the city where I would meet my wife and get ready for dinner. We ate at a little Italian restaurant that night, outside on the deck. As I sat there enjoying my meal, looking toward the mountain that had caused such suffering earlier, I thought, "what a strange day. At one time I am in a winter snow storm and the next moment, I am sitting outside having dinner". A season of changes, in a day.

Diligence: Chapter 2

*For the person of energy, thoughtfulness,
pure conduct, considerate action,
restraint, wholesome living, and diligence,
glory increases.*

*Diligent among the negligent,
ever vigilant among the sleeping,
the wise person moves on
like a swift horse
who has overtaken a weak one.*

*A practitioner delighting in diligence,
seeing dread in negligence,
being near to the unbinding
cannot likely fall away.*

Story 2: I loved racing in the mountains of Colorado. The one caveat to that is the race organizers would always seek out some of the most nasty climbs you can imagine. Especially if it was a circuit race, where you had to climb said nasty hill several times. However, this race was an out and back, so that meant that not only did you have to climb the same hill (or hills) twice, but in a different direction with totally altered pitches and climbing strategies. I was racing with the veterans, the 35 to 44 year old guys that were of all categories and some were ex-pros still hammering away at, well 35 to 44 years. Being a rather large stage race in the state, there were many categories of racers and they were all full with between 50 and 100 cyclists per category. Our starting time was a good 15 minutes in front of the women's Pro-1,2 category, the best of the females. Yet we were a fast bunch of some very fit vets and as stated earlier, a field with some accomplished racers. With all the climbs involved, it wasn't long before the field was split. I found myself with a few other individuals always pushing the pace to reduce the gap from the lead group that had dropped us on one of the climbs. We continued together but by the turnaround point, I was all alone in what is referred to as "no-man's land". That place where you have been dropped, you have dropped and are basically riding alone. This is somewhat difficult in that as you pedal by your lonesome, you try to keep a fast pace but it is hard to tell because there is no-one in sight to gauge whether you are gaining or losing ground. And then there is that zone-out point where you kind of look at the asphalt in front of your wheel and basically "zone-out". That is where I was when all of a sudden this little, blond female went powering by me. I tried to keep pace but to no avail. Are you kidding me? I can't keep up with that little girl. It was kind of humiliating but because of her power, there were no other females around to witness my lesson on being dropped. "Wow!" I thought. "That is one powerful little girl", although I knew she was an adult female, she really was small. I realized then that power can definitely come in small packages. I later learned that she was a national team rider for the Australian Olympic team and was using this Colorado race as a tune-up for the Olympics just a month away. As I watched the female Olympic road race later that summer, I witnessed this same girl blow away the competition and win the Gold Medal. My humiliation turned to awe and humbleness. I had been beaten by the best.

Mind: Chapter 3

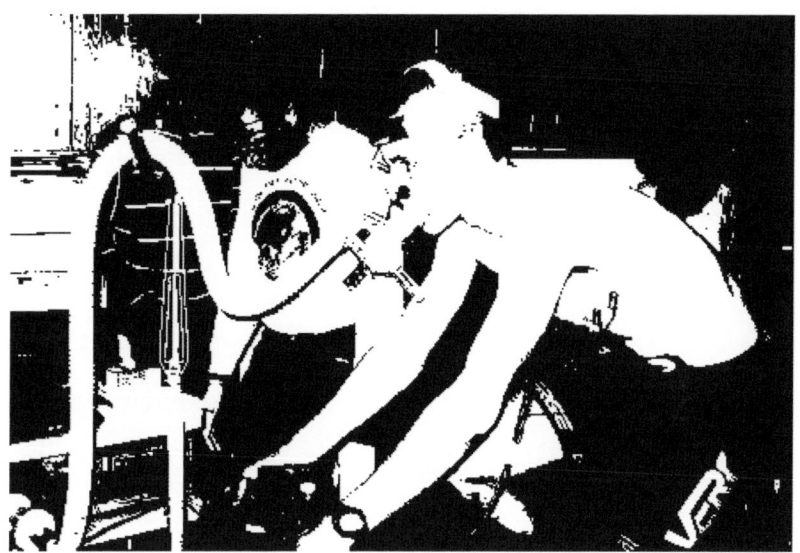

*There is no fear for the wide awake-
the one who has let go of gain and loss,
whose mind is not moistened by passion,
whose thoughts are un-assailed.*

*Whatever a rival may do to a foe,
or a vengeful person to the one he hates,
a wrongly applied mind would do more
damage to him than that.*

Story 3: The local race would take us through a valley surrounded by mountains. It was a slight grade uphill and at various points the pitch increased, would plateau and even slightly go down for a brief period. However, the majority of this race was uphill and it ended with a pretty good climb. With all of this in mind, it did not take long for the group to string out and those of ability moved to the front and those without were dropped. It is always interesting to me in these races that you find yourself surrounded by those of equal ability. A microcosm of the race. Sort of reminded me of society. Those of a certain socio-economic status surrounded by others of similar stature. The haves and have-nots. Such was the process of this race as I continued forward surrounded by those of similar abilities. The race eventually came to an end (as all races do) and we sat across our top tube exhausted from the ride. The eventual ride back would ensue and for the next few days the story-telling would run through the community with each of us describing our interpretation of the effort. It was at this time that I heard that another local cyclist was really trying to beat me. I found it fascinating that a competition was taking place without my knowing of it. Me, I thought. Why me? There were others much more gifted to aim for. I realized of course that it must have been one of my surrounding neighbors as we rode. One of the cyclists of similar abilities. A lot like society. Someone trying to keep up with the Joneses. And I was Jones.

Flowers: Chapter 4

*A seeker will master this earth,
this world of death and radiant beings.
A seeker will gather a well-taught verse on the way,
as a skilled gardener gathers a flower.*

*As on the road,
in a heap of discarded refuse,
there might be born a lotus
of perfumed fragrance,
pleasing to the mind,*

*so amid those beings,
common and blind,
who have become as refuse,
a disciple of the fully awakened one,
by means of insightful knowledge, shines.*

Story 4: It is not unusual to do a ride that starts one way and finishes another. To be clear, new rides in particular can be a surprise not only in their enjoyment, but in their torture. Thus it was for this particular ride in the state of Oklahoma. I had found a road that was considered a scenic highway, complete with website and facts. I called the individual listed on the website and asked if bicycles were allowed on this road. "Yes of course," she stated over the phone with a tone that indicated her pleasure to talk with anyone about the joys of this road. "I hope you are fit if you plan on riding this road on a bicycle", she ended the conversation. Little did she know how fit I was. So I did the ride. I experienced one of the most difficult rides I have ever done. I cannot express just how hard this ride was. I have ridden mountain passes in Colorado and even rode to the top of a 14,000 ft. mountain. While the hills I faced on this Oklahoma scenic highway were in no way of the elevation gain of the aforementioned "fourteener", they were many, they were relentless and they went straight up. I kept asking myself on this ride, "Don't these people know how to do switch-backs?" The answer was apparent. Straight up meant I did my own switch-backs across both lanes keeping a sharp eye out for traffic. A surprising ride on an unassuming highway in the heart land of America. I knew many of my cycling buddies would never believe me and I also knew they would never do this ride. I am a better man (and cyclist) for the torture this scenic ride provided me.

The Childish Person: Chapter 5

*That act is not beneficial which
having been committed, one regrets,
the fruit of which one receives
crying, face full of tears.*

*But that act is beneficial which,
having been committed, one does not regret,
the fruit of which one receives
pleased and content.*

*There is one way for acquiring things,
another leading to the unbinding.
Knowing this, the practitioner,
the disciple of the Buddha,
should not take pleasure in honor—
let him foster detachment.*

Story 5: The local races had been dominated by a team sponsored by one of the bike stores in this mountain community. Unfortunately, I was being sponsored by the competitive store but had no team-mates to counter the attacks of the dominant team. The upcoming race was a beautiful ride through a valley along a mountain river frequented by fly-fishermen that eventually hit several climbs skirting a lake and finishing at a small (very) community at lakeshore. The dominant team, while not large at generally four or five members, worked well together and it showed in their wins. The community had bike races every Tuesday night for any and everyone and had been doing this for years. It was great fun as we basically all knew each other and most of time the races were very competitive. So it would be this night as we arrived at the starting point, unloaded our bikes and basically prepared for battle. A friend of mine that I often trained with was there and as I approached him he smiled and granted me his friendly acceptance. But my motivation was not to solidify our friendship. It was to establish an alliance for combating the dominant team. It was a simple strategy: he, being the better climber would allow me to cover all the breaks and perhaps throw in a few attacks before the climbing began. Then he would have to work against those that were left to challenge the hills. He beamed at my suggestion enthusiastically stating, "I was hoping we could do this one day". And with that, our alliance and battle plan had been set. We meandered along the river with the dominant team setting tempo. It was fast enough to drop the less-fit. We slipped into their draft knowing they did not have the power to shake us. A periodic attack would evolve but I had it covered. I also tested the waters with my own attacks but I always made sure they were never a 100% effort in case a counter-attack followed. A few times it did but to no avail. The climb was in sight and before I could assess when or where to launch the next attack, my friend took off actually shouting, "I'm going"! Of course nobody does this but my friend did and darn if it didn't shake up the remaining members of the dominant squad. They all scrambled to catch his break. I just stayed on their wheels wondering what the heck my friend was up to. We eventually bridged at the precise point at the base of the hill. Quickly noting my competitors' heavy breathing in their effort to catch my friend, I launched my 100% effort attack as the pitch of the climb went up. I opened a sizable gap that took the majority of the climb for them to close. Clearly spent as they reached me, I too was about to blow. Then my friend with a quick glance and smile in my direction, took off. Only two hung with him and they disappeared from sight. The rest of the race I played cat-and-mouse with one other rider left with me. I took him at the line with a final burst for fourth place. As I coasted to a stop beyond the finish line, my friend rode up with a huge grin on his face and I knew he won the day. The next day one of the members of the dominant team came up to me smiling and said, "Well done last night. You guys spanked us". It's good to race with friends.

The Skilled Person: Chapter 6

He would not associate with harmful friends.
He would not associate with the lowest of people.
So, you should associate with encouraging friends;
You should associate with the best of people.

Few are those among the people
who cross to the other shore.
The rest of humanity just runs about
on the bank right here before us.

But those people who follow the way
when the teaching is well proclaimed
will go to the other shore.
The realm of death is so hard to traverse.

Story 6: Friends come into our lives, leave their mark and then are gone. Some are lasting, most are not. This has been my experience as I follow my path. I was fortunate to cross paths with a professional cyclist in my early years of riding and racing. An exceptional athlete with the funniest wit that ultimately revealed his high level of intelligence. It was rare that I could be around him and not laugh. His was a unique perspective on life and his philosophical discourses were filled with humor and great depth. But here he was earning his living on a bicycle. He was proficient in many venues of cycling, primarily mountain biking. But he held his own in road races and also excelled in an American side-note of bike racing called cyclo-cross. "Cross" is big in Europe with cyclists earning six figures just to race cross. However, in the US only a small sub-culture raced cross and for those of us that did, the explanation was in the doing. It was unadulterated fun and pain. Along the Eastern slope of Colorado one could find multiple cross races on any given weekend in the Fall. As it happened, this day that I showed up to race in the old-guy division my friend shows up to race in the category listed as Pro-1,2, the highest level. Greetings and smiles at seeing each other were given and his pleasure at seeing me do this type of racing was evident. After removing my bike from the roof rack and donning my shoes and helmet it was time for me to warm up. In multiple category races as this the organizers generally have the lower level cyclists go first and proceed up the chain of command. My group was one of the first to go while my friend would wait most of the day before his category would race. I meandered around the course mounting and dismounting at barriers, practicing getting up to speed, maneuvering my bike over questionable terrain when I heard someone approaching me from behind. As I glanced back I noticed it was my friend. "Keep going" he shouted and I continued to move slowly through the course. However, at each barrier he would talk me through the procedures of how to dismount my bike and following the barrier, he would tell me how to remount. Throughout the course my friend was taking his time to tutor me on the nuances of cyclo-cross. Information that many would pay for was being given to me free of charge, without solicitation. He didn't have to do this. I didn't expect him to do this. But he did. Out of the kindness of his heart and the integrity of a man that supports his friends, even if they race in the lower categories. Many years later, this was a lesson I carry with me to this day, and a person I continue to call "friend".

The Accomplished Person:
Chapter 7

*There is no fever for the person
who has completed the journey-
free from sorrow,
freed in every respect,
the knots removed.

His impulses exhausted
and nutriments starved,
free, empty, and without conditions
is his sphere of action.
As birds in space, his way is hard to trace.

Calmed is the mind,
calmed, speech and action
of one set free by genuine knowledge.
For such a person
there is peace.*

Story 7: They say timing is everything. In Europe there are early Spring races referred to as the "Spring Classics". These are one day races set up in epic formats with names like, "Paris-Roubaix", "Fleche-Wallonne" and "Liege-Bastongne-Liege" to name a few. In Colorado there is an early Spring ride near where I lived, and it too was billed as a "Classic". A square circuit of 18 miles, the Master's group with which I raced was required to do 3 laps for a total of 54 miles. Nothing outstanding about this but it was near the Wyoming border and the winds were always a factor, as was the finish. While there were a few rollers on this course, the final 500m was one of these rollers with the crest of this incline acting as the finish line. Having done this race several times before, I realized that when turning one of the corners of this large 18 mile square the pace picks up and if you are not paying attention and the turn is into a head wind, you will quickly find yourself off the back, never to return to the group. The winds can be so decisive in this regard that even a few meters back of the group results in a futile struggle to maintain contact. This had happened to me in previous races here. Today was different. I played everything right sitting in when necessary and pulling hard at appropriate times. As it was, I found myself in the leading break of 12 cyclists for the majority of the race. We worked well together keeping our distance from the main pack with all of us realizing that a 12 man sprint held better odds than a pack sprint. So we continued to work as one until the final section that led up to the inclined finish line. The pace always quickens and few tried to break away without success. The finish line was in sight. However, I have come to realize that an uphill view is deceiving in the actual distance that is to be covered. I was sitting about five back from the leaders as they began their run-up to the final sprint. Then, all of sudden the "sea" parted. The leaders shifted to my left and there was no one in front of me. I took this opportunity to jump on my pedals and sprint for the line. Another optical illusion in cycling is that the closer you get to the finish line, the further it is. It seems to move away from you, as was the case this day. As the finish neared to the point that I could reach out and touch it, my quads tightened and I struggled to push the pedals. Then I saw in my peripheral vision two wheels inch their way in front of mine…at the line. The victory I tasted was snatched from me as I took third place this day. Had I started my sprint just a few meters later I am convinced I would have won. My timing was just a few seconds off, and it made all the difference. A few seconds. What a great race this was!

Thousands: Chapter 8

*Better than a thousand statements
composed of meaningless words
is a single meaningful word which,
having been heard, brings peace.*

*Better than a thousand verses
composed of meaningless words
is a single word of verse which,
having been heard, brings peace.*

*It is better indeed to conquer yourself
rather than other people.*

*Better than living a hundred years
lethargic, low in energy,
is a single day lived
exerting steadfast vigor.*

One day as a tiger.

Story 8: There were four of us on this ride. One of my favorite rides is called an out-and-back ride. Through a valley alongside a mountain stream, the out part ended at the top of a mountain pass with a formidable climb to get there. Of the four of us, I was in the bottom tier of abilities. One other was of similar ability but the other two were far better cyclists than I. This day was like every other day. It was beautiful, sunny and just cool enough to keep our body temperature at a reasonable point to allow for some fast riding without over-heating. We worked a nice four-man pace line through the valley. Each took a turn at the front for a small period of time then drifted to the side and the back of the line to allow the next to take their turn at pulling. We all knew what lay ahead and for the most part, the knowledge of the effort that would soon confront us kept the speed at a reasonable rate. No one pulled too long and no one pulled hard. We were conserving all we had to unleash our best effort on the climb. And then, it was before us. I liked this particular climb because it had a few switch-backs but they were separated by long stretches of gradual grade climbing. This of course meant that you could easily see those either in front of you or behind you with a quick glance. The gradual aspect of the climb around each switch-back played into my strengths as a climber in that my power was not off-set by my size. At just over six foot, I was considered big for a cyclist and really big compared to the pure climbers. On this day, no one really jumped to the lead at the beginning of the climb, but the steady pace dropped the rider, whose ability was close to mine, almost immediately. I rode on the wheel of the other two as we approached the second switch-back and at this point, I felt rather good. After the steep curve of the switch-back, I decided to push the pace, got out of my saddle and stood on my pedals. I wouldn't normally do this and even now the thought crossed my mind that I could be "cutting my own throat", as they say. But I threw caution to the wind and continued forward at my own even pace still standing on my pedals out of the saddle. The other two stayed with me for a while but gradually slipped behind. I actually climbed out of my saddle for several miles. And this is how it continued to the top, to the end of the out part where we all convened and re-grouped for the ride back. Nothing was said. We rode the back part (of the out-and-back) as a group again in a steady pace line. It was quiet all the way back, each of us lost in our own thoughts and concentration toward our immediate task. We pulled into the parking lot and dismounted our bikes. As we put the bikes back on our cars for the return trip home, a few low volume gestures of "good ride" quietly emerged from my fellow cyclists. And that is how it ended. One of my best rides ever. My most powerful and dominating climb ever. It ended in quiet resolve. Actions do speak louder than words.

Detriment: Chapter 9

*If a person does something detrimental,
he should not do it again and again.
He must not create that impulse in himself.
Pain is the accumulation of detriment.*

*If a person does something valuable,
he should do it again and again.
He must create that impulse in himself.
Ease is the accumulation of value.*

Story 9: I have trained on my bike in the mountains of Colorado, the hills of Kentucky, the piney woods of Northern Louisiana, Sun-baked terrain of North-Central Texas and the flat-lands of Kansas. Each holds its own level of difficulty and each has its own level of aesthetics. Some would guess that the more difficult rides from the choices above would be in the Colorado

Rockies. And they would not be wrong. Yet at each location that I find myself, I encounter a ride (or rides) that matches the highest level of difficulty of any ride I have done, anywhere. It is as though the elements come together along with characteristics of the ride that make for a most difficult ride. The perfect storm if you will. The characteristics may be the length of the ride, the speed of the ride, my level of fatigue in beginning the ride or a combination of all the above to provide me with yet another painful training session. Such was the case on many of my rides in the flat-lands of Kansas. I was teaching at a University that was situated on the North end of the city. As such, my rides always went North, so I could avoid the perils of city traffic and hit the country early for uninterrupted miles of riding. The saying in Kansas is not "is the wind blowing" but "how hard is the wind blowing"? You see, the wind is always blowing. On this particular ride it was in the late Fall, and Winter was right around the corner. And of course we all know that the cold wind comes from the North. But not this day. There was a tremendous wind right out of the South that had me flying as I headed in a Northerly direction out of town and away from the University. Any cyclist will tell you that to ride for miles with a tail-wind is a wonderful thing. Such power and speed with such little effort is a rare occurrence. I should have realized this as I looked down at my watch and realized two things: 1) I had been riding hard in a Northerly direction with a tailwind for just over an hour and; 2) I had less than an hour to get back for a class I had to teach. Less than an hour into a headwind covering the same distance I just went with a tailwind for over an hour. Now that is what is referred to as a training stimulus. Tucked on the drops and hammering in the big gear I basically time-trialed back to the university. The "characteristics" of the ride came together this day to provide the perfect storm: a horrendous head wind, fatigue, maintaining an aero position, pushing the big gears and of course, time. Utterly exhausted when I returned I made my lecture on time. The hardest ride I have ever done? The perfect storm I faced in the flat-lands of Kansas.

Violence: Chapter 10

*Whoever, through violence, does harm
To living beings desiring ease,
hoping for such ease himself,
will not, when he dies, realize ease.*

*Whoever does no harm through violence
to living beings desiring ease,
hoping for such ease himself,
will, when he dies, realize ease.*

*Do not speak harshly to anyone.
Those to whom you speak
might respond to you.*

*Angry talk really is painful.
The result might crash down on you.*

Story 10: Mountain biking is a different animal than road cycling. I believe there are more skills involved with keeping a bike moving steadily uphill while navigating a narrow path and dealing with surfaces that are less than ideal for tire traction. I have never been a good mountain biker and it is probably because I just do not do it that much. On this ride, a friend from out of town came to ride with me and he was a good mountain biker. So I decided to take him to some local trails. We had to ride our mountain bikes several miles prior to hitting the trails and this was fine as it provided some time for warm-up and good conversation. Once on the trails, the talking stopped and I had to concentrate to keep my momentum up the first climb. It is not unusual for me to come out of my pedal clips during a trail climb as I struggle to keep going straight, avoid large rocks and maintain some level of traction with my wheels. It gets frustrating and this is why I do not continue to pursue this venue of cycling. Yet I know with a little practice I could improve but I often choose the road primarily because I feel more competent on a road bike. My friend dropped me and that was fine. I did not want to hold him back with my incompetence. We continued to ride several hours and really had a good time. With his mountain bike needs met, we decided to head back to my house. Once again we were on the road that took us to the trail-head but the traffic was noticeably heavier. Now, part of this return trip involved going down a pretty substantial hill that also involved a 270 degree sweeping turn. As we made our way down this section of the return ride home, we found the cars pushing us to the outside of the road more and more. As I passed one car in particular, I made my displeasure of their location on the road known by verbally shouting for them to move over. Now realize that as one diverts their attention from the task at hand (in this case riding down and around) they tend to go straight rather than follow the curving road. In an instant, I was off the road headed into the ditch and before I could respond, I did what is commonly called, a "header": over the front of the handle bars and sprawled out in the ditch. My friend immediately came to my aid as did one of the drivers that witnessed the crash. As I sat up I did an inventory of body parts and all felt well. With a bruised ego and frustration at what just happened, we re-mounted our bikes and continued toward my home. However, as I rode with my friend following, I realized that this road I was on that I had ridden many times before, that I could probably ride in the dark on most occasions, was totally foreign to me. Nothing looked familiar. Perhaps, I thought, I should be more attentive to the moment.

Old Age: Chapter 11

*Worn out is this body,
a frail nest of disease.
This festering mass breaks apart,
for life has death as its end.*

*Even the colorful chariots of kings age.
The body, too, grows old.
But the way of those who are good
does not grow old,
for the good teach it
to those of fine character.*

Story 11: Individuals often ride with those of similar abilities. This makes sense in that if one were to ride with a lesser fit cyclist, they would have to wait. Conversely if one were to ride with someone considerably better, it would be discouraging and somewhat embarrassing to make that person continually wait. For many years I rode with an individual in this Colorado community that was really better than me, barely. On any given day if he was down a bit and I was up, I could take him. So our training together facilitated my quest to better him and his quest to never let that happen. It also happened that we became friends. This is bonus in that when your training partner is slightly better than you and your friend, you can be happy for him when he does bury you. Also, he will show genuine gratitude at your efforts to beat him. And so it was for several years over countless training rides and many, many miles together on the road. Once, we were on this ride that we often did out in the middle of nowhere. It was a good place to ride in that there were several bisecting roads that would allow us to alter our ride based on whatever whim we felt like following that day. We coursed through the country side and just happened to be in an area devoid of trees when my friend mentioned that "nature called". As it happened, I had to answer the call of nature as well. We pulled over to the side of the road, unclipped from our pedals, straddled our bikes and as they say, "whipped it out" to do what comes natural. "You watch in that direction and I will watch this way for cars" my friend shouted from a short distance. You never want to actually pee right next to your buddy. In fact, I do not like using urinals in men's restrooms as the proximity of the other attendee is too close for my comfort. As we continued on this desolate road without a soul in sight, as would be expected a car emerges from around the bend. Murphy's Law. "Car", I shouted followed by "hurry up" as I anxiously finished and replaced my exposed body part. Then I heard, "You don't understand. As a 50 year old male, you do not 'hurry up' pissing". We both started laughing as he just managed to finish before the car passed. And we continued to ride with lightness in hearts…and bladders.

Oneself: Chapter 12

*You are master of yourself.
What other master could there be?
It is by restraining oneself
That one attains the master-
So difficult to attain.*

*One should not neglect one's goal
for the goal of another, even if great.
Knowing well his goal,
let him be a person who pursues
the true goal.*

Story 12: Five of us wind our way through the paved trail surrounded by Aspen trees. The wind blows the leaves ever so gently giving one the impression of little hands randomly waving as we pass. This is our warm-up and a connection to a road where the real training will begin. We chat and move in a fluid fashion as the trail meanders beside a mountain stream. Such peace seems difficult to replicate. Why should I even care about wanting this experience over and over again? Probably because in the back of my mind I know it will never be replicated. Ah, the road up ahead is in sight. We turn right only to immediately face a substantial hill that must be climbed and before I know it, I am alone. Not in front, but behind. Of course I knew this would happen as the friends I ride with this day are very good cyclists. Now what? These individuals could have written the book on "survival of the fittest". For them, it is drop or be dropped. I was the latter. And these fellows would not wait at the top of the climb. This was not "The Way". Yet now, even in this most uncontrollable of situations I had a choice: suffer immensely or ride at a pace more suited to my level of cycling. One choice would allow for a pleasant ride and perhaps more insight into meditative "moments". The other would never be described as pleasant, and in fact would be rather unpleasant. One, some would surmise, would be chosen from intelligent thought and the fact that humans often seek states of homeostasis. The other, some might note, is the choice of masochists hell bent on disrupting the norm. Two choices. Little to ponder really. It seems obvious from the past that accomplishments and adaptations come not from remaining in the cocoon, but from pushing the boundaries. Altering the status quo. Changing environments, cellular phenotypes and even thought patterns that in the end, allow us glimpses of our true potential. Besides, pain is a good thing, right?

The World: Chapter 13

*Do not embrace an inferior way,
or live a life of negligence.
Do not embrace a wrong view,
or be a person who indulges in this world.*

*Better than sole sovereignty
over the earth, going to a higher world,
or dominion over the cosmos
is the fruit of entering the stream.*

Story 13: With every race there is a pre-race assessment of your competitors. I was racing cyclo-cross for the first time in 5 years so my assessment took on significant meaning in this field of 20 master's men and female racers. We cyclist do this not just to determine whom might beat us but to really determine whom we will beat and thus not come in last. I pegged two in this race that

I felt confident that I could beat: the fat guy and the girl. Surely I would beat these two. I don't mean to sound stereotypical in my assessment but I was a pretty fit guy and these two did not look like competition. But as the race began and the suffering continued lap after lap, I quickly noticed the fat guy was a good 200 meters in front of me. But where was the girl? As I glanced back during a flat section the answer surprised me. She was on my wheel! With each lap I would gain ground on the fat guy during the technical sections of the race only to lose it again during the long, flat section where he could out-power me. And the girl: we periodically switched leads. With two laps to go the fat guy gassed and I eventually caught him. The girl drifted back as I increased my speed upon reeling in the fat guy. And as the race ended, the fat guy and the girl did, indeed, finish behind me. My pre-race assessment was correct, barely. Or was it? And what did I learn? That I must be "the old guy" or "the fit looking guy that doesn't race fast" or some other label pegged on me prior to the race. Many finished in front of me this day. I finished behind many on this day.

The Awakened: Chapter 14

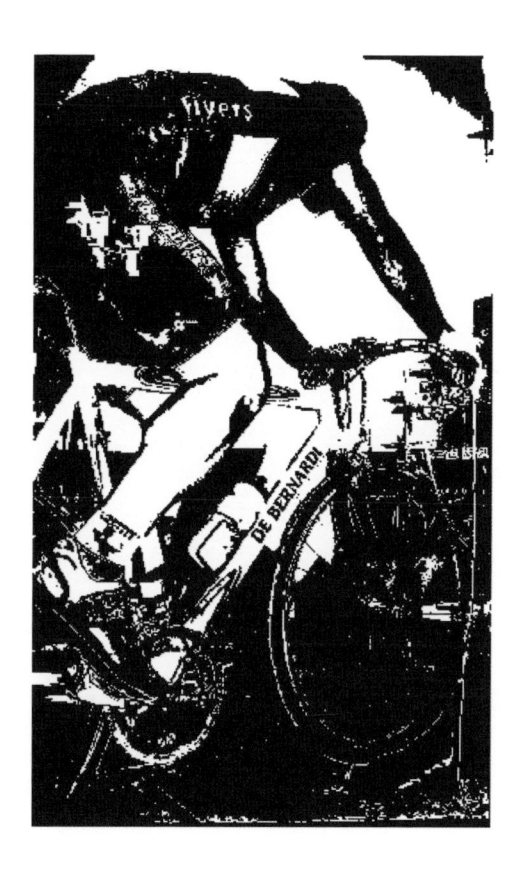

*They are wise who pursue meditation,
delighting in the calm of renunciation.
Even the radiant ones long for those
who are fully awakened, the mindful.*

*Not abusing, not harming,
restraint in line with the discipline,
moderation in eating and seclusion in dwelling,
exertion in meditation as well-
this is the teaching of the awakened.*

*An excellent person is rare;
one is not born just anywhere.
Wherever that wise one is born
the family abounds in happiness.*

Story 14: Many variables make for a difficult ride. Environmental conditions such as altitude, the pitch of the ride, the temperature, the wind. And then there are the internal factors such as fatigue level and psychological stress conditions at any particular time. It is the unexpected and unaccounted for factors that leave you shaking your head and laughing or shaking your head and crying. Either way, you are left shaking. I had been through the most traumatic injury in my life involving one of my knees. This is both physically and psychologically devastating to a cyclist. However, here I was back on my bike rehabbing my knee. This was the best rehab and I felt blessed that I loved my mode of rehab. This process began with just trying to obtain enough range of motion so I could complete a full pedal stroke. I knew in my heart, that if I could just get that full pedal stroke my rehab process would take off. And as it turned out, this was true. By the time I took this ride I had ridden a few weeks at twelve and fourteen hours per week on the bike. This week, I would hit sixteen total hours counting today's 2.5 hour ride. I was tired to begin with, but also mentally excited in that I was putting in hours on the bike this week that exceeded previous training weeks even before my injury. I was moving into new physiological territories and knew it was here that my adaptation would occur. As I began my ritual warm-up a fellow cyclist and his girlfriend passed me. This would not do. I picked up my pace, glued to their rear wheel and at the appropriate time, powered past the two of them. The male of course, gave chase but I had gapped him enough to realize if I maintained my current pace he would soon drop. And he did. Not without some considerable effort on my part. Enough so that I couldn't help but feel that perhaps the previous week's hours on the bike were taking their toll on my legs. No matter, I continued on my ride at my pace. I came to a cross-road on this ride and as I entered the intersection two cyclists going in my direction went by. This, again, would not do. I bridged to the rear wheel of the back rider and when the time was right, I again put distance between myself and the boys. These two didn't chase but their speed was enough that to continue my lead and hopefully extend it required yet another considerable effort. Not half-way through this ride and I was already near cooked. For several miles I continued at my own pace but now my pace seemed excruciatingly hard and slow. My legs were tired, my speed seemed slow and my mental edge and been dulled by the effort that now consumed my thoughts. I glanced back, only to see in the distance a lone cyclist. Damn! I picked up the pace. He or she never caught me but the days ride was turning into a hammer fest of my own making. Each time I stomped on the pedals the bike would not respond.

Thoughts of overtraining filtered across my brain but I soon realized that the only thing I could think of for any length of time was my damn fatigue. I was damned fatigued. But as always, I made it home. Slumped over the handle-bars I waited for the garage door to open so I could put the bike away and collapse. Then a thought crossed my mind. Not a good thought because it would reveal something in myself I did not want to face. But it was a thought all the same, one that I could not ignore and one that I could easily verify. I checked my front tire and sure enough it was mush. Like riding your road bike through a grassy field. And to make matters worse, as I spun my back wheel I realized I had ridden the whole ride with my brakes rubbing on the back wheel. My realization had been confirmed: I was an idiot. However, it was an effective training ride.

Being at Ease: Chapter 15

*Oh, with what ease we live
when peaceful amid the hostile!
Amid the hostile people
we live peacefully.*

*It is beneficial to see noble people.
In their company one is always at ease.
Not seeing childish people,
one would live in perpetual ease.*

*Firm, insightful, knowledgeable,
fastened to morality, devout, noble-
you should follow a person like this,
a good person possessing real wisdom,
like the moon follows the path of the stars.*

Story15: Deer hunting season in Colorado can be a scary time for cyclists. It is a time for breaking out your most colorful kit and hopefully, one that is bright orange or red. In fact, because of overly enthusiastic hunters the local ranchers tie red ribbons on their horses so they will not be mistaken for a deer and shot. Now how anyone can mistake a horse for a deer is beyond me but apparently it has happened and thus the adorned horses. It was during this time that I decided I wanted to ride up a dead-end road to the fish hatchery. I loved this ride because it took a considerable effort to get there, the scenery was beautiful and not many knew of this road so the traffic was minimal. I rode alone this day and as mentioned before, wearing my bright orange long sleeve jersey. There was a Fall nip in the air and as is often the case, the skies were clear as the sun shone and the blue was almost luminescent. This was a great day to ride. There was a good 25 miles of meandering road before one made it to the turn-off to the fish hatchery. From that turn it was a steady climb for several miles until the road would dead-end into a real fish hatchery. There were many twists and turns so you really could not see too far in front. As I made my way, I came around a corner to witness two hunters decked out in their own bright orange vests and hats. They were unloading their rifles from the back of a truck and as I passed, we made eye contact but not a word was said. Some people do not like cyclists on the road and I am not sure why. I think it may have to do with freedom and child's-play but I have never asked those that indicate their disdain as these two hunters did. I passed quietly.

Then, about 50 meters beyond the hunters around the next corner, I encountered yet another male. Only this one was a huge buck with a rack that anyone would be proud to wear. In the case of the hunters, a rack they would proudly display on their wall. But not this day. "Run," was all I could think of saying and after a quick glance in my direction, he was gone. Hidden in the brush with his own camouflage. I think my memory of that encounter will last longer than any display on someone's wall.

Pleasing: Chapter 16

*People hold dear the person
who is endowed with virtue and vision,
established in the teaching,
truthful in speech,
and who does the work that is his.*

*The person who would bring forth
a desire for the nameless, mind clear,
thought not enmeshed in sensual pleasures,
is called "one who is streaming upward."*

Story 16: Early in my racing career I traveled to a metropolitan area to do a criterium. A circuit course of short duration, hair-pin turns and shoulder to shoulder situations that provide for a lot of anxiety and excitement in this venue of racing. I did not particularly like criteriums but would later discover that I had a fair amount of success in this type of race venue. I arrived early to get my bike ready, warm up properly and prepare mentally for the high speed cluster that defines a crit. As I unloaded my bike I happen to notice another, fellow cyclist a few cars away with his bike already prepped, cycling kit and shoes on and literally stuffing himself with donuts and coke. The sight caught me by surprise and I almost laughed out loud as he shoved in those white-powdered donuts with a cola chaser. White powder down his front and across his face he noticed me looking and through muffled, donut-stuffed mouth a quick "hey" and nod of the head. Uh, "hey" was all I could muster. Wow, I thought, that guy must be nervous to put that much crap away. Well, good luck to you and I hope I am not around when that comes back up. The race began and as all crits begin it was fast and dangerous, especially in the corners. With a fast pace the field is strung out, thinned out and generally whittled down to the dozen or so that will sprint for the victory. After the initial weeding-out, the lead group settles into a rhythm around each circuit with constant lead changes. There is an ebb and flow as the speed increases, decreases, steadies and the process begins all over again.

High, low, steady, high, low, steady and then the race officials indicate there are three laps to go. Then, we all go. The speed continues to accelerate and with this the danger is amped up. Cornering becomes more treacherous, the group becomes more anxious and contact with those next to you is continual.

Everyone jockeys for position as we head into the final turn that will lead to the sprint. Position at this point can mean the difference between a victory and tenth place. Diving into the corner, wheels overlap and a few riders go down. The speed is such that you only look forward but you hear the devastation in metal and flesh on concrete. Out of the corner and out of the saddle I was stomping on the pedals for maximal power and a surge that would carry me to the line. And out of nowhere, "Donut-Boy" shot ahead with a sprint that no one could match. He won! Donut-Boy won! I came to realize this particular person was one of the best sprinters in the area. And obviously, with a little sugar kick, he could do some damage. My new pre-race meal: donuts and cola.

Anger: Chapter 17

*The person who can restrain
anger that has arisen
like a reckless chariot-
that one I call a driver.
Other people just hold on to the reins.*

*Win over an angry person with poise.
Win over a mean one with kindness.
Win over a greedy person with generosity,
and one who speaks falsely with honesty.*

*Those gentle sages,
constantly restrained in body,
go to that unshakable place where,
having gone, they do not suffer.*

Story 17: My mind wanders as I ride. I assume this is true of most cyclists when they ride alone. I choose to ride alone but I am not adverse to riding with a group. I think I prefer the lone ride because it does allow me to think and ponder the meanings of life. I have found that these "thoughts" flow and sometimes the sequence of thoughts are quite bizarre. This day my thoughts are rooted in my ability to love those that have hurt me and provide tolerance to those that would hurt me. This is a difficult task, I believe, but seems to be a common theme in spiritual writings. Buddha expressed the need for tolerance, love and compassion toward our fellow man. Jesus tells us to love our enemies and turn the other cheek when confronted. I am convinced, as I ride, that this takes a stronger person than any sort of retaliatory action or similar action to those that would do us harm. Very difficult indeed. As I ride and my mind ponders these wonderful lessons I sense a love and compassion in my own heart. My ride nears the end as I approach an underpass. I must stop, momentarily at the stop sign that precedes the underpass. I continue at a considerably slower pace when a pick-up truck going in the opposite direction slows. As it does so the window goes down (I do not notice this) and a young man shouts out, "Dick-head"! My loving self shoots him the finger and shouts back "F- -k you, A- -hole!" Without the blanks in between. It occurs to me that I may have just failed a test.

Toxins: Chapter 18

*More toxic than rust
Is ignorance, the greatest toxin.
Eliminating this toxin,
Be flawless, you practitioners!*

*There is no path in space.
There is no seeking externally,
Fabrications are not eternal.
There is no agitation in awakened ones.*

Story 18: I ride up the mountain in a rhythmical fashion straining on the pedals yet able to maintain some resemblance of even force output. It is important in cycling to do this. Maintain an even road allows for efficiency and reduced loss of energy. It is important to stay relaxed in areas not associated with force output to the pedal as this only exacerbates energy loss which in cycling, can come back to haunt you later in the ride. I think a lot when I ride. Now I am thinking, "what an interesting analogy this ride is turning out to be. My actions at the beginning of the ride will have consequences to the later part of my ride." Karma. Of course all of this will manifest itself within hours which allows me to see the connection between early efficiency and later energy output. I like that. Most humans would. Our attention span as a species is generally short and our patience seems even shorter. By establishing a Buddhist concept that plays out in a matter of hours makes me smile as I continue up this mountain. If only other Karmic acts were so noticeable (I am thinking). Then that jerk that honked at me thirty minutes ago is probably experiencing some sort of gastric distress or perhaps he got caught running a red light or some other mishap (I am thinking). Justice (I am thinking). Unlike my pure and spiritual self, my good acts of exercise on the bike will pay dividends to a healthy body later on (I am thinking). Yes I will in fact be better off (later on) because of this ride I currently face. Right now it is freaking painful as the incline increases and "where the hell did that head wind come from" (my thinking has been disrupted). I burp and indigestive gas release from the pot of coffee I downed before the ride and I no longer am enjoying this ride. A deer sits just off the road grazing with it's fawn and the crisp morning air moves the Aspen leaves as if to applaud my efforts. I do not see any of this because in my effort to push myself up this mountain my eyes are glued to the asphalt in front of me. That freaking cold air hurts my lungs and I quickly ponder why I didn't start this ride later when the temperatures would be more moderate. I know why: I wanted to get this over with. I near the end of the ride as I see the crest. Why do distances seem to extend themselves as we near the end and our efforts are so substantial (thinking again)? Einstein karma I suppose. But the ride does end as I slump over my handle bars coasting on the small patch of flat terrain at the crest of this challenge. I clip out of my pedals and straddle my bike to take in some water and the scene before me. Beautiful (I think)! I feel "one" with the Universe. I am in the moment. I feel thankful and humble. Is this enlightenment (I think)? My mind wanders off the moment and toward the descent. This descent is going to be freaking cold (I think), with future thoughts of my warm house and yet another cup of hot coffee. I have experienced struggle and reached the top, of this mountain anyway. Am I there yet? Time to descend.

Firmly on the Way: Chapter 19

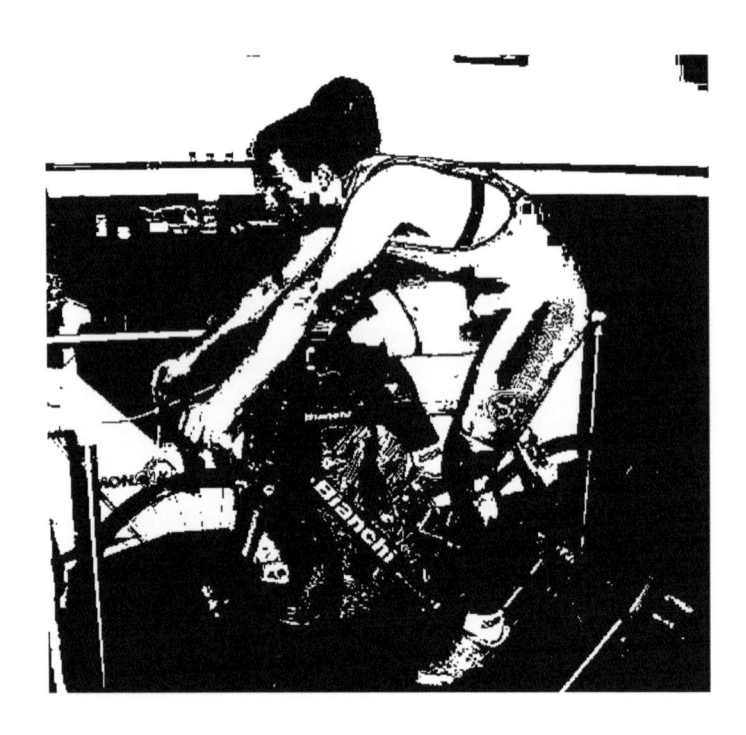

*But a person in whom there is
truthfulness, morality, gentleness,
restraint, and self-control-
that person, toxins dispelled, wise,
is called "venerable".*

*But whoever stills negativity
coarse or subtle, in every way,
because of the stilling of that negativity,
that person is called a "seeker".*

Story 19: Difficulties in cycling come in many different forms.

Mountains, the pace of the ride and even the distance one

covers becomes an exponential adverse affect. But for this ride,

the difficulty was unseen yet felt continually. I speak of the wind.

Any and more than likely, every cyclist will tell you that when cycling, you are always riding into a head wind. Well there are head winds and there are head winds. For this ride, anyone (even those driving in their cars) would recognize that the wind on this day was formidable. To add to this difficulty, half of the ride would be directly into this wind. Many curse the wind but I do not. I embrace this unseen force. I have come to realize that the wind is a metaphor for many struggles faced in life. Unseen, felt, in your face, relentless, yet at times, forgiving. On the bike I knew the wind only made me stronger. It forced me into an aerodynamic position. It was my competition and as such, I had to use a strategy when I faced it. Because half of this ride was going against this invisible foe, I always chose to face my nemesis when I was fresh…during the first part of the ride. I do this regularly and each time I start out mentally throwing down the gauntlet: "give me your best shot". Before I reach the turn-around point I have suffered, and cursed, and verbally pleaded for some respite. But to no avail. The wind is unfeeling. The wind does not give in to my pleas. The wind is a true friend. Because the wind knows that as it increases its challenge in the face of my fatigue, I will only benefit from its detached involvement in my development as a cyclist. And as a true friend will do, the wind will pick me up when I am most down. Ah, the return trip back has begun.

The Path: Chapter 20

*From practice springs
expansive understanding;
from lack of practice, its loss.
Being aware of this divided pathway
to cultivation and decline,
conduct yourself so that understanding increases.*

*Tear out your self-regard
as you would an autumn lily with your hand.
Foster only the path to peace, to unbinding,
taught by the one who traveled it well.*

Story 20: One aspect of meditation that is extremely difficult for me is to quiet the internal dialog. It seems as though the blank mind I seek to achieve, is next to impossible. Knowing this, the great teachers of the past realized we must focus on a sound, a mantra during the times we stray from quiet to dialog in our meditation. Thus the sound and word of "Ohm" as this signifies the collective sounds of the Universe. As I ride my bike I find my mind wanders to many past, and possible future scenarios. To be without thought is, once again, next to impossible for me. So I decided on this ride to fill my senses with as much of the Universe as I could within the moment. I wanted all information to come into my awareness unfiltered as though a child absorbing the material for the very first time. I broadened my visual awareness, opened my ears to all sounds, tried to smell any and everything and basically overload my senses. What I discovered was astounding. First, with this much information coming in it was nearly impossible to have an internal dialog. I could not think about past situations, conversations, future possibilities, worries or anything. I had to work to take it all in but it really was not difficult. The difficulty was in sustaining this level of sensory acceptance. But the other realization I came to was a complete surprise. For any given moment and during all moments that I was "taking it all in", a bird or birds were always part of my experience. There was not a time that a bird was not within my senses. I either saw a bird or heard a bird at all times. Birds provided an intricate link from one species to another that could not be avoided. And why should it be avoided? It was a pleasant lesson in some level of symbiotic relationship.

Scattered Themes: Chapter 21

*The faithful person, endowed with virtue,
possessing wealth and fame,
to whatever place he resorts,
there he is honored.*

*Good people illumine from afar,
like the snowy Himalaya.
Those who are not good
are unperceived here,
like arrows shot in the night.*

Story 21: Often during training rides my mind wanders to the greater meanings in life and the Universe. Do we receive messages throughout the day (or ride) that we are totally clueless to? I would be open this day to any messages that came my way. Perhaps a bird singing intently on the telephone pole beside the road. Or a rare glimpse of a coyote in the field during the daylight hours. Or that Bobcat I see near the trail by the lake, that shows no sign of fear of my approach. None of these would happen today but they have in the past. Were they messages then? I stayed open to the possibilities. As I approached a cross street I notice two young females walking in my direction. With my keen powers of observation I surmised they were out for a fitness walk as they both had water bottles, were both a little obese and both seemed intent on the walk, not the scenery. What was a bit odd is that they were about 30 yards apart. As I crossed the street I decided to allow them an encouraging word in hopes of providing motivation for continued walks and increased health. "Good morning", I chimed as I crossed the road in front of the first female. A quick eye-contact then she turned her head without a reply. What the hell? Perhaps it wasn't a good morning. I kept riding with a bit of a pissed off attitude at what I had just experienced. So, is this my message from the Universe today? "Do unto others…but they will not return the kind gesture to you". I kept riding. Several miles later with a stop-sign quickly approaching I noticed out of the corner of my eye (as well as heard) a truck slowing right beside me following my pace. Without looking (so I wouldn't crash) I prepared myself for the worst: some insult, some object thrown, another message from the Universe. "How far are you riding," came the query from the driver of the truck? "Oh, probably about 40 miles today" I ventured. "I did ten this morning" he beamed. We continued to slow as the stop sign came closer. "Well" I stated, "that is about 10 more than most people out there". He laughed as did I. "Hey," he shouted "you ever need water, I live just back down the road and you are welcome anytime you see my truck there". "Thanks," was all I could say. It is sometimes hard to respond when the Universe is talking to you. Mixed messages are often not mixed at all, just our interpretation of them.

The Lower World: Chapter 22

*As grass that is hard to grasp
cuts the hand itself,
the seeker's life mishandled
pulls one down to the lower world.*

*For any inattentive act,
for an inconsistent practice,
or a dubious religious life
there is no abundant fruit.*

*If something is to be done,
one should proceed firmly.
The inattentive practitioner
is more scattered than the dust.*

Story 22: If you ride the roads long enough, regardless of where you live, eventually you will encounter dogs. Now I understand the territorial aspect of dogs but when they venture outside their yards (i.e., their territory) and onto the road, then I get testy. I have tried many deterrents to the chasing packs including the following: pepper spray (better have good aim and do not wipe your sweaty brow with the hand that sprayed); rocks (should have a good throwing arm and I do but to continually hold onto rocks while you ride is a hassle); kicking (you have to unclip and have many skills for this one such as good balance, good aim and the ability to stay on your side of the road while executing this maneuver). The kick would be my only option on this ride as I had no pepper spray nor had I picked up any rocks. I was riding early because I had a flight out of town with a colleague to go to a national conference. I wanted to get my ride in knowing there were several days of no-riding while I was at the conference. The route was a familiar one and generally free from attacking dogs. There was one area that a dog would periodically chase me but only if he was out and only if it was not too hot for him to exert himself. Well, he was out and it was fairly cool this morning so the conditions were optimal for him to chase. However, I was caught unaware of his looming presence because just before I entered his domain, my colleague called on my cell phone. I reached back in my cycling shirt pocket, extracted my phone and began our conversation pertaining to the trip. Then I saw him. Approaching at a very fast speed I knew he would intercept me based on his angle, my speed and his speed. We were on a collision course. Quickly I stated to my colleague, "hang on, a dog is coming" and I grabbed my handle bars, unclipped my shoe from the attack side and at the precise moment, threw a kick to the jaw of the dog. "Nailed You" I shouted! And the dog immediately slunk back to his place under the shade of his master's car. As I put the phone to my ear, all I could hear was the hysterical laughter of my friend. "I heard it all" he stated and we laughed together. That dog has never chased me again.

Elephant: Chapter 23

*Certainly, not with these vehicles
could a person go to the unreached realm,
as a trained person goes
with restraint, with good self-control.*

*Delight in diligence!
Watch over your mind!
Pull yourselves out of misfortune
like an elephant, sunk in mud.*

*A comfort is virtue into old age.
A comfort is the establishment of conviction.
A comfort is the attainment of insightful knowledge.
Not acting destructively is a comfort.*

Story 23: The ride totaled 98 miles. I would climb over two mountain passes with one topping out at 12,000 ft. I would descend at over 50 mph with hairpin turns. I would ride a slight grade uphill into the wind for over 40 miles. The final descent into my destination would be on a paved trail where I could meander to the hotel where my wife had already reserved a room. She would find me after this most difficult ride, in a bathtub soaking away my fatigue. It was an opportunity to ride. My wife was attending a professional workshop in her field of work at a mountain resort approximately 98 miles from where we lived. I knew the route as I had driven it in the car many times. But driving in a car one misses the little things such as slight uphill grades, rollers and of course head-winds that seem to last forever. But I saw the opportunity and seized it. I was well aware that it would be a difficult ride but of course we can never know the extent of adventures until we are fully immersed within them. Riding this kind of distance alone is another fear I had to overcome. No one to work with during those long head-wind stretches. No one to pace me when my mind wandered and the road seemed to stretch into infinity. No one to offer support if a flat or lack of water add to the obstacles that you have to overcome. I was all alone in this ride. But this did not deter me. No, it facilitated an even greater effort to finish the ride. Of course in my mind, it confirmed my resilience in facing challenges and emerging victorious. I feel that I have done this much of my life. Such was my mind-set and high level of confidence when a fellow cyclist that knew of my adventure offered me this comment when I returned home a few days later; "I was sure you would quit". Who offers this kind of sentiment? Obviously, someone that does not know me.

Craving: Chapter 24

*But whoever overcomes this miserable craving,
in this world so hard to overcome,
sorrows fall away from him,
like a drop of water from a lotus blossom.*

*Let go of the past!
Let go of the future!
In the present, let go!
Gone to the other shore of becoming,
mind released entirely,
you will never again undergo
birth and old age.*

*Free from craving, not grasping,
skilled in the interpretation of sentences,
he would understand the assemblage
of the words, from first to last.
He who has his final body,
possessing vast wisdom,
is called a "great person."*

*The gift of the teaching surpasses every gift.
The flavor of the teaching surpasses every flavor.
Delight from the teaching surpasses all delight.
The dissolution of craving conquers every pain.*

Story 24: When I travel in the car with family I always have my bike on the roof-rack. Always looking for opportunities to ride a different terrain in a new region of the country is exhilarating. As we traveled through Colorado on this trip we came to an area I was very familiar with. However, what made this opportunistic ride different was that it traversed a mountain pass on the back-side of a mountain that I had been up before only on the front side. As I unloaded the bike I really did not know what lay in front of me for my ride up this pass, but I knew what was on the other side, the front side. I would meet my family at the bottom of the "front side" in a small mountain village. It was a beautiful day as I said my good-byes and began my long climb up the "back side" of this mountain pass. There were several switch-backs in the beginning as I gained elevation with each turn. The large pine trees dwarfed those of us seeking adventures on this road and at the same time provided me with plenty of shade on this solar day. That would change. Many know that as you gain elevation and the partial pressure of oxygen is reduced, the flora changes considerably. In fact, there is a point called the "timber-line" where trees cease to exist. Only low lying foliage, grasses and flowers grace the terrain. This is where I was when I encountered a surprise visitor. There was a slight drop on the opposite side of the road away from the shoulder of the road. As

I struggled climbing in my saddle, I could gaze to the opposite side of the road and actually not see what was immediately next to it. Then, seemingly out of nowhere, a huge head appeared. It was the size of my complete torso. Luckily, it was a herbivore species. A large cow Elk. Curious, I suppose, at my panting from my efforts, she seemed to just look up to see what was happening. Totally surprised, I said my "hello" and continued up the mountain pass. A reminder that others, more adept in this environment, were willing to share it with me.

The Practitioner: Chapter 25

*The practitioner whose mouth is controlled,
Who discusses the texts unassumingly,
explaining both the meaning and the spirit-
sweet is that one's speech.*

*Even if he has achieved but little,
A practitioner should not demean
his own achievement.
The radiant ones praise that person
for his pure and vigorous life.*

*Thoroughly mastering the rise and fall
of the aggregates, from whatever source,
he attains delight and joy.
For those who understand,
this is the deathless.*

Story 25: While the mileage was not that great, the climb was epic. I started from an elevation of 8,000 ft. and by the time I reached the top I would be at 12,000 ft. Needless to say, this would take some time and of course, effort. I loved this ride. It seemed to have a life of it's own. On a climb like this, there were different slopes at various points and even a few flat sections. But the flat sections were very few. Through these various sections the efforts, the challenges and the eventual successes seemed to provide a different story that I could play out each time I made this ride. Adding to the storyline were factors such as the weather. This could be sub-categorized into temperature and wind. The time of year always made a difference. If I went in the Spring the early snow melt filled the adjoining river and at times was deafening as it flowed over fallen boulders. Local and visitor traffic provided color commentary whether in the form of admiration for my efforts or in a more derogatory manner because I slowed their progress. And of course, my fitness level was the greatest factor in how the story of the climb would unfold. This is always the case. The epic stories are not so much about the factual encounters that take place, but rather about how individuals handle these encounters. I never quit on this climb regardless of my conditioning. I suffered on this climb, regardless of my conditioning. It was evident to me that while weather conditions, or seasonal differences, or the level of traffic always factored into the ride, my approach and involvement in this ride were what made it epic. On this day, I once again was on an epic ride. On this day, as I rode the last few miles above timber-line, as the partial pressure of oxygen diminished and I struggled to keep pace, I knew in my heart I would finish. It was cold this high up and I felt the bitter wind on my face as I made the final turn. I pushed to the end, the summit. There was a smattering of individuals taking in the views from the summit. More than a few attentively watched as I drifted into the parking lot and slumped over my handle-bars. A portly man moved away from his RV and approached. Did he seek my wisdom? Was he astounded by my epic adventure? What insightful question would he ask? "Hey, did you ride that thing up here"? Epic.

The Superior Person: Chapter 26

*For whom neither the far shore nor the near,
nor both the far and near, exists,
that person, free from fetters and distress,
I call superior.*

*Meditating, sitting clearly,
doing what had to be done,
free from the impulses,
the highest goal attained,
that person I call superior.*

*The person who is not afraid,
having severed every tie,
transcending attachments, free,
that one I call superior.*

*The innocent person who endures
insult, physical harm, and imprisonment,
whose strength is forbearance
-the strength of an army-
that one I call superior.*

*The person who understands pain
dissolving it in this life by himself,
who has put down the burden and is free,
that one I call superior.*

*The person who has lain down violence
toward sentient beings-plants and animals-
who neither kills nor causes to kill,
that one I call superior.*

*The person who is harmonious amid the hostile,
peaceful amid the violent,
free from grasping amid the greedy,
that one I call superior.*

*The person for whom there are no expectations
concerning either this world or the world beyond,
who is without wishing, free,
that one I call superior.*

*The person for whom there is nothing
in the beginning, middle, or end,
who, having nothing, is free from grasping,
that one I call superior.*

*The person who is fearless, excellent,
heroic, a great sage, victorious,
free from desire, cleansed, awakened,
that one I call superior.*

Story 26: Birthdays are special. In my adult life I have tried to tie in some sort of physical challenge on my birthday in October. Nothing really formal and especially no formal invitations to the aforementioned challenge. One year I induced a group of students to do a fitness challenge for 44 minutes to commemorate my 44 years of life. One year I chose to do a substantial climb up a small mountain 5 times for each decade of my life. Generally, when I throw down these challenges I try to link a positive cause to the physical feat. This year, I decided to do a "Ride for Peace". With the United States in two wars and the political parties at each other's throats, I thought the theme of peace was appropriate. Weeks before I sent the word out that I was planning my birthday "Ride for Peace" in a local mountain range. Not an extremely hard ride but definitely a challenging one. The ride would include a circuit of 24 miles done twice and a final hill climb up a prominent peak. One unexpected challenge to the 24 mile circuit was a set of switch-backs that had a killer pitch. All in all a challenging ride. But the effort was for a good cause. Word of mouth spread and I periodically would receive an email or call expressing interest in joining me in this ride. The plan was to meet at a local gas-convenience store in the early morning hours to get started. In October it was excellent riding weather, generally begun with arm warmers that would soon be removed. I was anxious and excited as I waited in the parking lot that morning not knowing exactly who would show. And I waited. And I waited some more. Time passed and I soon realized that this might turn out to be a solo ride. It did. I did the ride alone. A beautiful ride that challenged my abilities as I had hoped. I finished atop the peak and asked a young man that had driven his car up the peak, to take my picture. As I stood there exhausted from the ride, I hoped that somehow my ride would allow for a little more peace in the world. The young man with the camera asked if I was ready. I smiled and gave two hand signals: Peace and Love.

Biking IS my religion!

Afterword

Frank Wyatt's Buddha on a Bike hits the nail on the head in it's subtitle: "Stories of an enlightened-cyclist wannabe." More importantly, Frank cuts to the chase, getting down to the nitty, gritty core of one of the best kept secrets of East Asian Buddhism is expressed as soku shin jo butsu (即身成佛): enlightenment/awake is this very body/embodiment. That expression likely doesn't make a lot of sense since it's not just cryptic, but more so challenges bridging two very different cultures in quest of an integrative understanding of what the words Buddha, enlightenment, body, and their identification might mean. Our traditional Western culture holds mind and body to be separate. What a puzzle that poses. Since the late 19th century, Western science has favored an account of life based on reducing mind and feelings to material causes in the brain. That view is known as epiphenomenalism, and claims that just as our kidneys produce urine, our brains excrete consciousness as a by-product, perhaps a waste product — insofar as consciousness is trivialized as a byproduct or side effect of brain operations. Buddhism is a troublesome word since it cannot be translated with any sense of meaning into Pali, Sanskrit, Chinese, Tibetan, or Mongolian — the five official canonical languages of "Buddhism". Buddhism is an early 19th century invented word, one foreign colonialists and pioneering explorers from Western civilization figured would do the deed in making sense of a non-Western tradition. When they coined the term "Buddhism", they assumed those folks they branded as Buddhists held to some sort of beliefs characterizing their outlook and behavior. After all, among Christians, the gating question informing unique outlooks is 'what do you believe in?" In other words, what dogma do you adhere to for membership in a system of beliefs likely coloring and distorting your primary raw experience of life?

My entry into Awakeism (an appropriate rendering of Buddhism) stemmed from athletic training — from pro wrestlers incorporating Japanese judo and contemplative techniques to sharpen peak performance. Thanks to those guys, my graduate education was in a Japanese Buddhist institution, with a fellowship in Japan deepening training, eventually resulting in passing experiential exams resulting in board certification as a Kyoshi, akin to a Zen roshi, some 40 years ago. I didn't undertake such training in order to accumulate foreign beliefs in order to 'stink of religion.' Bottom line was a journey to an integrative understanding of our hidden, dormant, yet natural, perhaps genomic, basis for peak performance as human beings unencumbered by culturally imposed limiting dogmas.

The Awakeists claim that normal human understanding is mumyo (無明), meaning literally "not bright" or "unillumined" — not sin or alienation. The first step for overcoming mumyo is shoken (正見), habitually and inappropriately translated as 'right views.' Both shoken and the original Sanskrit samyak drsti deserve attention. Sho/samyak means making whole, full, complete, implying not bright is a condition of incomplete, fragmented understanding. Ken/drsti means 'seeing, views, or world view,' Hence the moral sense of 'righteousness' is not implied since the task is one of experientially filling in the blanks to get the whole picture so we get it right in understanding. Beyond theory, grist for the mill in Awakeist agendas aims at shugyo (修行), or gaining mastery. More helium filled words? Mastery of what? Disciplines freeing us from the bonds of membership in socially accepted dogmas limiting genomic or natural expression, disciplines of freedom accentuating peak performance. Where the rubber meets the road.

Epilogue

One Man's Journey

I was introduced to competitive cycling by a friend. A guide if you will. These guides surface from time to time in the most unexpected ways. They are adults, children, males and females. They are animals both wild and domestic and they are…everywhere.

After my introduction to bicycle racing, I should have looked elsewhere for a competitive outlet and perhaps for a new friend. My introduction to cycling could certainly not be viewed by many as a "good" experience. My first race was a time trial that was disastrous in epic proportions. Other cyclists sarcastically remarked of the poor quality of my equipment. I almost missed my start and then actually fell over prior to being released by one of the officials. Laughter ensued by those witnessing my first attempt at a time trial. It was physically painful as most time trials are. My time was…dead last among all the competitors. And yet, I left that day exhilarated from the experience. This occurred on a Tuesday and by Saturday, I had purchased a new bike. We must ask ourselves as we journey through this life if the roadblocks are there for denial of that particular path, or to strengthen us in our resolve to resume along that path.

A historical analysis of my athletic endeavors would reveal an individual that was successful in team sports and in particular, those that involved a ball. From an early age (6 y), I succeeded in sports. This was in part, an outcome of growing up in a family enmeshed in watching sports as well as an older brother that excelled in sports. Based on this brief description of my early athletic career, it might seem surprising to the outside observer that I would be totally "hooked" on a sport that is seemingly isolated (i.e., one-on-one, mano-a-mano) relying on a high degree of endurance rather than explosive physical output. But if one were to delve even deeper into the nuances of the aforementioned childhood sports that I was involved with, they would see that while baseball is indeed a team sport, the position I excelled in was that of pitcher: rather isolated on the mound. Additionally, the position I chose for football was that of quarterback. Again a bit of an isolated position based on the sport's requirement of that position involving strategy and responsibilities. Interestingly, the formidable challenges that cycling offered were not psychological in nature, but purely physical. I had never attempted a sport in which I did not excel…until now. I have often wondered if we, as a species, choose paths that are fraught with hardship to challenge our essence and make hard our resolve? Or are we just ignorant?

The journey for anyone with motivation is one of determination, sacrifice and laser-sharp focus. This was my life for many years pertaining to the sport of cycling. Of course, many will recognize these same attributes toward any goal. A high level of motivation is the driving force of their actions. Whether it involves making vast amounts of money, obtaining an educational degree or pursuing the love of your life: motivation toward a goal…can consume you.

As I ride and train I often find myself with others of similar competitive nature. In cycling it is all about riding someone off your wheel when the competitive spirit takes over. During my early years these training sessions often left me alone on the ride as I contemplated exactly how I could eventually close that gap. Early on, I was the one that was continually dropped. My initiation to cycling was with a group of individuals that were not only gifted cyclists, but also competitive. Theirs was a mind-set of everyone having to pay their dues. This of course meant that any new person attempting to partake in "their" sport must prove worthy. A typical response to anyone ever whining about being dropped was to "get stronger and keep up". Problem solved. And so, I often found myself riding solo on what began as a group ride. It was during these times that self-reflection fired the majority of synapses within my brain. However, an odd thing happened to those synaptic firings during high intensity, competitive endeavors: they cease to exist. I believe it has something to do with pain and suffering.

Suffering is inevitable on the bike. I have often heard it said that successful cyclists know how to suffer. Knowing how to suffer seems a strange concept as I believe we as a species, all know how to suffer. Our mothers suffer through our birth. We suffer through the pains of growing. If you have ever lost at love, you know the emotional suffering that ensues. Suffering is not a foreign concept to humans. Suffering, it could be argued, is inherent to our growth. I believe this. So, what is suffering? In some Buddhist translations suffering is unhappiness. In cycling, it is a level of physical discomfort that goes by many names: blowing up, exploding, knackered and of course, pain. It is, in fact all of these things. Appropriate terminology. So let us get past the fact that all humans "know" how to suffer. What is different with cyclists is that this inherent physical pain known as suffering is an everyday occurrence that is embraced. As a cyclist you know before the ride ever begins that pain and suffering will be part of the process. When the course is laid out you are keenly aware of when and where the suffering will begin. There is an awareness of the level of suffering you will endure and you have a pretty good idea of how long this suffering will last. Amidst all of this speculation on when and where and how intense the suffering will be resides, an ever-deeper consciousness cyclists own: they personally, will be responsible for inflicting the pain that so many will suffer through, including themselves. It is a stage in every cyclist's journey that they must be responsible for increasing the pace, the speed, the tempo to a level that requires those that follow to suffer. This is the ultimate embrace of suffering in the saddle. To be responsible for inflicting pain to others and oneself is the step toward removal of the negative connotation of suffering and acceptance of the joy that comes from suffering. It is, in a moment of time, the essence of Yin and Yang.

As I continued to ride and train through the years it was quite evident in the physical sense that one had to suffer to become "better" at cycling. Physiologically, it is a demanding sport. Hours, days, months and years of time in the saddle often yield minimal results. Yet however minimal, results just the same. Results in this sense are signs of moving forward. Suffering became another name for necessity as it related to moving forward in cycling. It was necessary to push into pain and suffering zones to achieve the adaptations needed for improvement. Perhaps, it is that way with most things: job advancement, earning an educational degree, remaining in a relationship for a length of time. These all require a level of pain and suffering to achieve a higher level. As humans, we suffer to obtain enlightenment. Buddha (Siddhartha) certainly did. But he also realized in his state of enlightenment that what he was seeking, was there all along. It is within us to achieve, to move forward. Suffering and pain are inherent to this achievement. They are components of achievement that are not to be avoided. In suffering, we find ourselves outside the sphere of comfort that leads us to new levels. As we suffer, we are secure in the fact that the peak of the mountain we climb is not far away.

      I ride my bike a lot. Day upon day, week after week, the years unfolding before me. The bike is my refuge. Each time I glide out of the driveway I know I am on a journey. A journey with a certain amount of predictability.   Yet at the same time a completely unknown outcome lies before me. It is an escape into a normal world where the future is uncertain. My ride strengthens me physically, mentally, emotionally and spiritually. It makes me a complete human. For a few hours a day my body, mind and spirit can behave as they were meant to behave. As I continue this process each day, the physical, mental and spiritual part of me becomes finely tuned. The outside influences of our world that are detrimental to my existence fade away. They have no influence on my life as I continue to ride: day upon day, week after week, the years unfolding before me.

Every journey is unique. Everyone's journey is their own. All journeys transform an individual in minute increments, or overwhelming epiphanies. Each morning as we awaken, a new life has begun. Each night as we drift into unconsciousness, as in death we enter into an unworldly state. A beginning, middle and end. A life lived in a 24 hour time span. Day upon day, week after week, the years unfolding before….

The journey I have taken, the journey I am on and the journey that awaits me is…your journey. Each day when we wake we live a new life. Each week we are transformed into a new being. Each year is but another time element of an existence that knows no boundaries. I will ride my bike tomorrow, and through the week, and for years to come. But first, I must awaken.

Thank you!

Dr. Frank B. Wyatt

Author Biography

Frank B. Wyatt

Dr. Frank B. Wyatt received a Bachelors of Science in Education from The University of North Texas, a Masters of Arts in Physical Education from San Francisco State University and a Doctorate of Education in Exercise Physiology from The University of Northern Colorado. He has published over 30 articles in scientific journals, presented over 75 research presentations at professional meetings and has worked in the fitness industry for over 30 years. He is currently a Full Professor in the Department of Athletic Training & Exercise Physiology at Midwestern State University in Wichita Falls, Texas. He is a member of the American College of Sports Medicine (ACSM), the National Strength and Conditioning Association (NSCA), the American Society of Exercise Physiologists (ASEP) and The International Council for Health, Physical Education, Recreation, Sport, and Dance (ICHPER-SD). His current research involves myocardial fatigue during endurance events and the adaptation response of cyclists to high intensity work output. Dr. Wyatt continues to cycle over 200 miles per week. In addition, he is a 4th Degree Black Belt in Taekwondo.

Printed in Great Britain
by Amazon